D0229614

OUR
FAMILY HISTORY

'There is a history in all men's lives.'
WILLIAM SHAKESPEARE,
KING HENRY IV PART II

EBURY PRESS STATIONERY

Family memories are precious – too precious to be left to chance. A personal record of your family history and activities will help to keep important events fresh in your mind.

In this book you will find sections in which to record details of all the members of your family – parents and grandchildren, brothers and sisters, uncles, aunts and cousins, your own descendants. You can chronicle their births and marriages, their occupations and activities. There is space to write about pets and holidays, homes and heirlooms, and to record the exciting events, achievements and crises that your family has survived together.

If you want to find out more about your family history, talking to older relatives is a good way to start. Encourage grandparents to reminisce about their younger days, and about their own parents and grandparents. If you are seriously interested in tracing your family tree, pin them down as to dates and places. Ask them to show you photographs and documents such as birth and marriage certificates.

Records of all births, marriages and deaths in England and Wales since 1837 are held at the General Register Office, St Catherine's House, Kingsway, London WC2B 6JP; those for Scotland at the Scottish Record Office, P. O. Box 36, HM

General Register House, Edinburgh EH1 3YY. The next phase of your research will take you to one of these offices. You can search the indexes for birth certificates, which will show the names of the baby's parents, then look for the parents' birth certificates and so on back through the generations.

Going back beyond 1837 is more difficult and may involve searching individual parish registers. However, many of these have been published, so you may not have to travel round the country and wade through massive handwritten volumes. The Society of Genealogists, 37 Harrington Gardens, London SW7 4JX, has the best specialist library in the country; you can do your research there or, for a fee, they will do it for you. There are also a number of regional genealogical societies which will be especially useful if your family has lived for a long time in the same area.

Finding out more about your ancestors can be more than just a hobby. It can give you a sense of security and continuity, answering basic questions about where you came from and where you belong. Record your findings in this book and add to it throughout your life. By writing about your own experiences as they happen, you will create a unique and truly personal heirloom to pass on to your children and grandchildren.

OUR IMMEDIATE FAMILY

GRANDPARENTS ON OUR MOTHER'S SIDE

_____

_____

_____

_____

GRANDPARENTS ON OUR FATHER'S SIDE

_____

_____

_____

_____

MOTHER

_____

_____

FATHER

_____

_____

CHILDREN

_____

_____

_____

_____

_____

_____

OUR FAMILY TREE

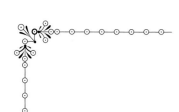

HUSBAND'S FATHER'S FULL NAME _____

HUSBAND'S MOTHER'S FULL NAME _____

DATE OF MARRIAGE _____

PLACE OF MARRIAGE _____

CHILDREN _____

_____

_____

_____

_____

HUSBAND'S FULL NAME _____

WIFE'S FULL NAME _____

DATE OF MARRIAGE _____

PLACE OF MARRIAGE _____

CHILDREN _____

_____

_____

_____

_____

'I can trace my ancestry back to a protoplasmal primordial atomic globule. Consequently, my family pride is something inconceivable.'

W. S. GILBERT, THE MIKADO

WIFE'S FATHER'S FULL NAME _____

WIFE'S MOTHER'S FULL NAME _____

DATE OF MARRIAGE _____

PLACE OF MARRIAGE _____

CHILDREN _____

_____

_____

_____

HUSBAND'S PATERNAL GRANDFATHER'S FULL NAME

HUSBAND'S PATERNAL GRANDMOTHER'S FULL NAME

DATE OF MARRIAGE   PLACE OF MARRIAGE

CHILDREN

HUSBAND'S MATERNAL GRANDFATHER'S FULL NAME

HUSBAND'S MATERNAL GRANDMOTHER'S FULL NAME

DATE OF MARRIAGE   PLACE OF MARRIAGE

CHILDREN

WIFE'S PATERNAL GRANDFATHER'S FULL NAME

WIFE'S PATERNAL GRANDMOTHER'S FULL NAME

DATE OF MARRIAGE   PLACE OF MARRIAGE

CHILDREN

WIFE'S MATERNAL GRANDFATHER'S FULL NAME

WIFE'S MATERNAL GRANDMOTHER'S FULL NAME

DATE OF MARRIAGE   PLACE OF MARRIAGE

CHILDREN

HUSBAND'S GREAT GREAT GRANDFATHER'S FULL NAME

HUSBAND'S GREAT GREAT GRANDMOTHER'S FULL NAME

HUSBAND'S GREAT GRANDFATHER'S FULL NAME

HUSBAND'S GREAT GREAT GRANDFATHER'S FULL NAME

HUSBAND'S GREAT GRANDMOTHER'S FULL NAME

HUSBAND'S GREAT GREAT GRANDMOTHER'S FULL NAME

HUSBAND'S GREAT GREAT GRANDFATHER'S FULL NAME

HUSBAND'S GREAT GREAT GRANDMOTHER'S FULL NAME

HUSBAND'S GREAT GRANDFATHER'S FULL NAME

HUSBAND'S GREAT GREAT GRANDFATHER'S FULL NAME

HUSBAND'S GREAT GRANDMOTHER'S FULL NAME

HUSBAND'S GREAT GREAT GRANDMOTHER'S FULL NAME

HUSBAND'S GREAT GREAT GRANDFATHER'S FULL NAME

HUSBAND'S GREAT GREAT GRANDMOTHER'S FULL NAME

HUSBAND'S GREAT GREAT GRANDFATHER'S FULL NAME

HUSBAND'S GREAT GRANDFATHER'S FULL NAME

HUSBAND'S GREAT GREAT GRANDMOTHER'S FULL NAME

HUSBAND'S GREAT GRANDMOTHER'S FULL NAME

HUSBAND'S GREAT GREAT GRANDFATHER'S FULL NAME

HUSBAND'S GREAT GREAT GRANDMOTHER'S FULL NAME

HUSBAND'S GREAT GRANDFATHER'S FULL NAME

HUSBAND'S GREAT GREAT GRANDFATHER'S FULL NAME

HUSBAND'S GREAT GRANDMOTHER'S FULL NAME

HUSBAND'S GREAT GREAT GRANDMOTHER'S FULL NAME

HUSBAND'S GREAT GREAT GRANDFATHER'S FULL NAME

HUSBAND'S GREAT GREAT GRANDMOTHER'S FULL NAME

WIFE'S GREAT GREAT GRANDFATHER'S FULL NAME

WIFE'S GREAT GREAT GRANDMOTHER'S FULL NAME

WIFE'S GREAT GRANDFATHER'S FULL NAME

WIFE'S GREAT GREAT GRANDFATHER'S FULL NAME

WIFE'S GREAT GRANDMOTHER'S FULL NAME

WIFE'S GREAT GREAT GRANDMOTHER'S FULL NAME

WIFE'S GREAT GREAT GRANDFATHER'S FULL NAME

WIFE'S GREAT GREAT GRANDMOTHER'S FULL NAME

WIFE'S GREAT GRANDFATHER'S FULL NAME

WIFE'S GREAT GREAT GRANDFATHER'S FULL NAME

WIFE'S GREAT GRANDMOTHER'S FULL NAME

WIFE'S GREAT GREAT GRANDMOTHER'S FULL NAME

WIFE'S GREAT GREAT GRANDFATHER'S FULL NAME

WIFE'S GREAT GREAT GRANDMOTHER'S FULL NAME

WIFE'S GREAT GRANDFATHER'S FULL NAME

WIFE'S GREAT GREAT GRANDFATHER'S FULL NAME

WIFE'S GREAT GRANDMOTHER'S FULL NAME

WIFE'S GREAT GREAT GRANDMOTHER'S FULL NAME

WIFE'S GREAT GREAT GRANDFATHER'S FULL NAME

WIFE'S GREAT GREAT GRANDMOTHER'S FULL NAME

WIFE'S GREAT GRANDFATHER'S FULL NAME

WIFE'S GREAT GREAT GRANDFATHER'S FULL NAME

WIFE'S GREAT GRANDMOTHER'S FULL NAME

WIFE'S GREAT GREAT GRANDMOTHER'S FULL NAME

Great, Great, Great Grandparents

Mr and Mrs	Nee
Mr and Mrs	Nee
Mr and Mrs	Nee
Mr and Mrs	Nee
Mr and Mrs	Nee
Mr and Mrs	Nee
Mr and Mrs	Nee
Mr and Mrs	Nee
Mr and Mrs	Nee
Mr and Mrs	Nee
Mr and Mrs	Nee
Mr and Mrs	Nee
Mr and Mrs	Nee
Mr and Mrs	Nee
Mr and Mrs	Nee
Mr and Mrs	Nee

Mr and Mrs	Nee
Mr and Mrs	Nee
Mr and Mrs	Nee
Mr and Mrs	Nee
Mr and Mrs	Nee
Mr and Mrs	Nee
Mr and Mrs	Nee
Mr and Mrs	Nee
Mr and Mrs	Nee
Mr and Mrs	Nee
Mr and Mrs	Nee
Mr and Mrs	Nee
Mr and Mrs	Nee
Mr and Mrs	Nee
Mr and Mrs	Nee
Mr and Mrs	Nee

'So for the mother's sake
the child was dear,
And dearer was the
mother for the child.'
SAMUEL TAYLOR COLERIDGE,
SONNET TO A FRIEND WHO
ASKED HOW I FELT WHEN
THE NURSE FIRST PRESENTED
MY INFANT TO ME

MOTHER'S FAMILY DETAILS

MOTHER'S FULL NAME

_____

_____

DATE OF BIRTH

_____

WAS BORN AT

(TIME) _____ (PLACE) _____

_____

PARENTS' FULL NAMES

_____

_____

SHE GREW UP IN

_____

_____

_____

WENT TO SCHOOL/COLLEGE AT

_____

_____

_____

INTERESTS AND HOBBIES

_____

_____

_____

OCCUPATION AND JOB DETAILS

_____

_____

_____

MET (NAME OF HUSBAND)

AT

DATE

THEY GOT ENGAGED

'Brightly dawns our wedding day;
Joyous hour, we give thee greeting!'

W. S. GILBERT, THE MIKADO

THEY GOT MARRIED ON   DATE

AT

BRIDESMAIDS/ATTENDANTS WERE

'You don't object to an
aged parent, I hope?'

CHARLES DICKENS,
GREAT EXPECTATIONS

MOTHER'S PARENTS' DETAILS

GRANDMOTHER'S FULL NAME

_____

(NEE)

DATE AND PLACE OF BIRTH

_____

_____

BROTHERS AND SISTERS

_____

SHE GREW UP IN

_____

EDUCATION/OCCUPATION/INTERESTS

_____

_____

_____

_____

GRANDFATHER'S FULL NAME

_____

_____

DATE AND PLACE OF BIRTH

_____

HE GREW UP IN

_____

EDUCATION/MILITARY SERVICE RECORD/OCCUPATION/INTERESTS

_____

_____

_____

_____

THEY MET AT   (DATE) _____

GOT ENGAGED   (DATE) _____

MARRIED (DATE)   AT _____

_____

_____

_____

GRANDPARENTS' BROTHERS' AND SISTERS' DETAILS

NAME

DATE AND PLACE OF BIRTH

OCCUPATION

MARRIED   ON

CHILDREN

NAME

DATE AND PLACE OF BIRTH

OCCUPATION

MARRIED   ON

CHILDREN

NAME

DATE AND PLACE OF BIRTH

OCCUPATION

MARRIED   ON

CHILDREN

'Parentage is a very
important profession.'

GEORGE BERNARD SHAW,
EVERYBODY'S POLITICAL WHAT'S WHAT

Father's Family Details

Father's Full Name

_____

_____

Date of Birth

_____

Was Born at

(TIME) _____ (PLACE) _____

_____

Parents' Full Names

_____

_____

He Grew Up in

_____

_____

_____

Went to School/College at

_____

_____

_____

Interests and Hobbies

_____

_____

_____

Occupation and Job Details

_____

_____

_____

MET (NAME OF WIFE)

AT

DATE

THEY GOT ENGAGED

THEY GOT MARRIED ON   DATE

AT

BEST MAN/USHERS WERE

'And the moral of that is –
'Oh, 'tis love, 'tis love,
that makes the world go round!'

LEWIS CARROLL, ALICE IN WONDERLAND

Father's Parents' Details

GRANDMOTHER'S FULL NAME

_____

(NEE)

_____

DATE AND PLACE OF BIRTH

_____

_____

BROTHERS AND SISTERS _____

_____

SHE GREW UP IN _____

_____

EDUCATION/OCCUPATION/INTERESTS _____

_____

_____

_____

GRANDFATHER'S FULL NAME

_____

_____

DATE AND PLACE OF BIRTH

_____

HE GREW UP IN

_____

EDUCATION/MILITARY SERVICE RECORD/OCCUPATION/INTERESTS

_____

_____

_____

_____

THEY MET AT   (DATE) _____

GOT ENGAGED   (DATE) _____

MARRIED (DATE)   AT _____

_____

_____

_____

GRANDPARENTS' BROTHERS' AND SISTERS' DETAILS

NAME

DATE AND PLACE OF BIRTH

OCCUPATION

MARRIED   ON

CHILDREN

NAME

DATE AND PLACE OF BIRTH

OCCUPATION

MARRIED   ON

CHILDREN

NAME

DATE AND PLACE OF BIRTH

OCCUPATION

MARRIED   ON

CHILDREN

'Ah! happy years!
once more who would
not be a boy?'

GEORGE GORDON BYRON, LORD BYRON,

CHILDE HAROLD

'The world has no such
flowers in any land,
And no such pearl in any
gulf the sea,
As any babe on any
mother's knee.'

ALGERNON CHARLES SWINBURNE,

PELAGIUS

CHILDREN

FULL NAME

WAS BORN ON   AT

WEIGHT

SCHOOL/COLLEGE/JOBS

FULL NAME

WAS BORN ON   AT

WEIGHT

SCHOOL/COLLEGE/JOBS

FULL NAME

WAS BORN ON   AT

WEIGHT

SCHOOL/COLLEGE/JOBS

FULL NAME

WAS BORN ON   AT

WEIGHT

SCHOOL/COLLEGE/JOBS

FULL NAME

WAS BORN ON   AT

WEIGHT

SCHOOL/COLLEGE/JOBS

FULL NAME

WAS BORN ON   AT

WEIGHT

SCHOOL/COLLEGE/JOBS

'Youth is the time to go flashing
from one end of the world to the other
both in mind and body... to hear
the chimes at midnight; to see
sunrise in town and country;
to be converted at a revival ...'

ROBERT LOUIS STEVENSON, VIRGINIBUS PUERISQUE

Grandchildren and Descendents

FULL NAME

DATE/TIME/PLACE OF BIRTH

PARENTS

FULL NAME

DATE/TIME/PLACE OF BIRTH

PARENTS

FULL NAME

DATE/TIME/PLACE OF BIRTH

PARENTS

FULL NAME

DATE/TIME/PLACE OF BIRTH

PARENTS

FULL NAME

DATE/TIME/PLACE OF BIRTH

PARENTS

FULL NAME

DATE/TIME/PLACE OF BIRTH

PARENTS

FULL NAME

DATE/TIME/PLACE OF BIRTH

PARENTS

FULL NAME

DATE/TIME/PLACE OF BIRTH

PARENTS

FULL NAME

DATE/TIME/PLACE OF BIRTH

PARENTS

FULL NAME

DATE/TIME/PLACE OF BIRTH

PARENTS

FULL NAME

DATE/TIME/PLACE OF BIRTH

PARENTS

FULL NAME

DATE/TIME/PLACE OF BIRTH

PARENTS

Aunts, Uncles and Cousins

AUNT (FULL NAME) _____

_____ (NEE) _____

DATE AND PLACE OF BIRTH _____

_____

UNCLE (FULL NAME) _____

DATE AND PLACE OF BIRTH _____

DATE AND PLACE OF MARRIAGE _____

CHILDREN _____

_____

_____

_____

AUNT (FULL NAME) _____

_____ (NEE) _____

DATE AND PLACE OF BIRTH _____

_____

UNCLE (FULL NAME) _____

DATE AND PLACE OF BIRTH _____

DATE AND PLACE OF MARRIAGE _____

CHILDREN _____

_____

_____

AUNT (FULL NAME)

(NEE)

DATE AND PLACE OF BIRTH

UNCLE (FULL NAME)

DATE AND PLACE OF BIRTH

DATE AND PLACE OF MARRIAGE

CHILDREN

AUNT (FULL NAME)

(NEE)

DATE AND PLACE OF BIRTH

UNCLE (FULL NAME)

DATE AND PLACE OF BIRTH

DATE AND PLACE OF MARRIAGE

CHILDREN

Aunt (full name) _____

(nee) _____

Date and Place of Birth _____

_____

Uncle (full name) _____

Date and Place of Birth _____

Date and Place of Marriage _____

Children _____

_____

_____

_____

Aunt (full name) _____

(nee) _____

Date and Place of Birth _____

_____

Uncle (full name) _____

Date and Place of Birth _____

Date and Place of Marriage _____

Children _____

_____

_____

'Four ducks on a pond,
A grass-bank beyond,
A blue sky of spring,
White clouds on the wing:
What a little thing
To remember for years –'

WILLIAM ALLINGHAM,
A MEMORY

GRANDPARENTS REMINISCE

Looking back over the years, one realises the changes that have taken
place in the world – new inventions, world events, fashions, trends, opinions.
It is the little details from your childhood that will interest your
grandchildren and their children. Here is the space to share those memories.

'The days may come, the days may go,
But still the hands of mem'ry weave
The blissful dreams of long ago.'

GEORGE COOPER, SWEET GENEVIEVE

'Reminiscences make one feel so deliciously aged and sad'
GEORGE BERNARD SHAW, THE IRRATIONAL KNOT

'To complain of the age we live in, to murmur at the present possessors of power, to lament the past, to conceive extravagant hopes of the future, are the common dispositions of the greatest part of mankind'

EDMUND BURKE, THOUGHTS ON THE CAUSE OF THE PRESENT DISCONTENTS

'I have had playmates, I have had companions,
In my days of childhood, in my joyful school days, –
All, all are gone, the old familiar faces.'

CHARLES LAMB, THE OLD FAMILIAR FACES

KENILWORTH CASTLE.

PARENTS REMINISCE

Here is your chance to put the record straight. What music did you dance to?
How much was a trip to a cinema? What are your strongest memories of growing up?

'Twopence a week, and jam every other day'
LEWIS CARROLL, THROUGH THE LOOKING GLASS

'And the brass will crash,
And the trumpets bray,
And they'll cut a dash
On their wedding day.'

W. S. GILBERT, THE MIKADO

FAMILY WEDDINGS

BRIDE

BRIDE'S PARENTS

GROOM

GROOM'S PARENTS

DATE AND PLACE OF MARRIAGE

BEST MAN, BRIDESMAIDS, USHERS AND ATTENDANTS

GUESTS

BRIDE

BRIDE'S PARENTS

GROOM

GROOM'S PARENTS

DATE AND PLACE OF MARRIAGE

BEST MAN, BRIDESMAIDS, USHERS AND ATTENDANTS

GUESTS

BRIDE

BRIDE'S PARENTS

GROOM

GROOM'S PARENTS

DATE AND PLACE OF MARRIAGE

BEST MAN, BRIDESMAIDS, USHERS AND ATTENDANTS

GUESTS

BRIDE

BRIDE'S PARENTS

GROOM

GROOM'S PARENTS

DATE AND PLACE OF MARRIAGE

BEST MAN, BRIDESMAIDS, USHERS AND ATTENDANTS

GUESTS

BRIDE

BRIDE'S PARENTS

GROOM

GROOM'S PARENTS

DATE AND PLACE OF MARRIAGE

BEST MAN, BRIDESMAIDS, USHERS AND ATTENDANTS

GUESTS

BRIDE

BRIDE'S PARENTS

GROOM

GROOM'S PARENTS

DATE AND PLACE OF MARRIAGE

BEST MAN, BRIDESMAIDS, USHERS AND ATTENDANTS

GUESTS

*'To have and to hold from this day forward,
for better for worse, for richer for poorer,
in sickness and in health, to love and to cherish,
till death us do part, according to God's holy
ordinance; and thereto I plight thee my troth.'*
BOOK OF COMMON PRAYER

BRIDE

BRIDE'S PARENTS

GROOM

GROOM'S PARENTS

DATE AND PLACE OF MARRIAGE

BEST MAN, BRIDESMAIDS, USHERS AND ATTENDANTS

GUESTS

BRIDE

BRIDE'S PARENTS

GROOM

GROOM'S PARENTS

DATE AND PLACE OF MARRIAGE

BEST MAN, BRIDESMAIDS, USHERS AND ATTENDANTS

GUESTS

BRIDE

BRIDE'S PARENTS

GROOM

GROOM'S PARENTS

DATE AND PLACE OF MARRIAGE

BEST MAN, BRIDESMAIDS, USHERS AND ATTENDANTS

GUESTS

BRIDE

BRIDE'S PARENTS

GROOM

GROOM'S PARENTS

DATE AND PLACE OF MARRIAGE

BEST MAN, BRIDESMAIDS, USHERS AND ATTENDANTS

GUESTS

BRIDE _____

BRIDE'S PARENTS _____

GROOM _____

GROOM'S PARENTS _____

DATE AND PLACE OF MARRIAGE _____

BEST MAN, BRIDESMAIDS, USHERS AND ATTENDANTS _____

_____

GUESTS _____

_____

BRIDE _____

BRIDE'S PARENTS _____

GROOM _____

GROOM'S PARENTS _____

DATE AND PLACE OF MARRIAGE _____

BEST MAN, BRIDESMAIDS, USHERS AND ATTENDANTS _____

_____

GUESTS _____

_____

'There is only one religion,
though there are a hundred
versions of it.'
GEORGE BERNARD SHAW,
PLAYS PLEASANT AND UNPLEASANT

RELIGIOUS OCCASIONS

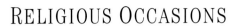

CHRISTENINGS, FIRST COMMUNIONS, CONFIRMATIONS, BAR MITZVAHS

NAME

OCCASION   (DATE)

PLACE

GODPARENTS/SPONSORS

NAME

OCCASION   (DATE)

PLACE

GODPARENTS/SPONSORS

NAME

OCCASION   (DATE)

PLACE

GODPARENTS/SPONSORS

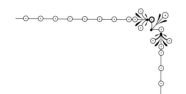

NAME

OCCASION _____ (DATE) _____

PLACE

GODPARENTS/SPONSORS

⁂

NAME

OCCASION _____ (DATE) _____

PLACE

GODPARENTS/SPONSORS

⁂

NAME

OCCASION _____ (DATE) _____

PLACE

GODPARENTS/SPONSORS

NAME

OCCASION   (DATE)

PLACE

GODPARENTS/SPONSORS

NAME

OCCASION   (DATE)

PLACE

GODPARENTS/SPONSORS

NAME

OCCASION   (DATE)

PLACE

GODPARENTS/SPONSORS

NAME

OCCASION   (DATE)

PLACE

GODPARENTS/SPONSORS

NAME

OCCASION   (DATE)

PLACE

GODPARENTS/SPONSORS

NAME

OCCASION   (DATE)

PLACE

GODPARENTS/SPONSORS

NAME

OCCASION   (DATE)

PLACE

GODPARENTS/SPONSORS

NAME

OCCASION   (DATE)

PLACE

GODPARENTS/SPONSORS

NAME

OCCASION   (DATE)

PLACE

GODPARENTS/SPONSORS

NAME

OCCASION   (DATE)

PLACE

GODPARENTS/SPONSORS

NAME

OCCASION   (DATE)

PLACE

GODPARENTS/SPONSORS

NAME

OCCASION   (DATE)

PLACE

GODPARENTS/SPONSORS

In Memory

'Tho' lost to sight, to mem'ry dear
Thou ever wilt remain.'

Song attr. to George Linley

'He marks – not that you won or lost –
But how you played the game.'

GRANTLAND RICE, ALUMNUS FOOTBALL

ACHIEVEMENTS OF CHILDREN

Every child has special moments of achievement as they pass through
childhood. These may occur at school, in sport, with particular hobbies or
talents, clubs etc. They may win prizes or take part in special events
or outings. Here's your opportunity to record these occasions for posterity.

'Almost everything that
is great has been done
by youth.'

BENJAMIN DISRAELI,
EARL OF BEACONSFIELD,
CONINGSBY

'As a decrepit father
takes delight
To see his active child
do deeds of youth.'

WILLIAM SHAKESPEARE,
SONNETS

'I have heard of a man who had a mind to
sell his house, and therefore carried a piece
of brick in his pocket, which he shewed as a
pattern to encourage purchasers.'

JONATHAN SWIFT,
THE DRAPIER'S LETTERS, No.2 (4 AUG 1724)

HOMES WE HAVE LIVED IN

ADDRESS

FROM   TO

IMPROVEMENTS/EXTENSIONS

PRICE BOUGHT   PRICE SOLD

OUR NEIGHBOURS WERE

'The house of everyone is to him as his castle and fortress.'
SIR EDWARD COKE, SEMAYNE'S CASE

ADDRESS

FROM   TO

IMPROVEMENTS/EXTENSIONS

PRICE BOUGHT   PRICE SOLD

OUR NEIGHBOURS WERE

'I remember, I remember,
The house where I was born,
The little window where the sun
Came peeping in at morn...'

THOMAS HOOD, I REMEMBER

ADDRESS

FROM   TO

IMPROVEMENTS/EXTENSIONS

PRICE BOUGHT   PRICE SOLD

OUR NEIGHBOURS WERE

ADDRESS

FROM   TO

IMPROVEMENTS/EXTENSIONS

PRICE BOUGHT   PRICE SOLD

OUR NEIGHBOURS WERE

FAMILY PETS

NAME

TYPE/BREED

COLOUR/APPEARANCE

HE/SHE WAS PART OF THE FAMILY FROM   TO

NAME

TYPE/BREED

COLOUR/APPEARANCE

HE/SHE WAS PART OF THE FAMILY FROM   TO

NAME

TYPE/BREED

COLOUR/APPEARANCE

HE/SHE WAS PART OF OUR FAMILY FROM   TO

*'Animals are such agreeable
friends – they ask no questions,
they pass no criticisms.'*

GEORGE ELIOT,
MR. GILFIL'S LOVE-STORY

NAME

TYPE/BREED

COLOUR/APPEARANCE

HE/SHE WAS PART OF THE FAMILY FROM   TO

NAME

TYPE/BREED

COLOUR/APPEARANCE

HE/SHE WAS PART OF THE FAMILY FROM   TO

NAME

TYPE/BREED

COLOUR/APPEARANCE

HE/SHE WAS PART OF OUR FAMILY FROM   TO

Family Holidays

PLACE

DATE

WHO WAS THERE

WHAT WE REMEMBER

PLACE

DATE

WHO WAS THERE

WHAT WE REMEMBER

PLACE

DATE

WHO WAS THERE

WHAT WE REMEMBER

PLACE

DATE

WHO WAS THERE

WHAT WE REMEMBER

PLACE

DATE

WHO WAS THERE

WHAT WE REMEMBER

PLACE

DATE

WHO WAS THERE

WHAT WE REMEMBER

'These are not dark days: these are great days – the greatest days our country has ever lived; and we must all thank God that we have been allowed, each of us according to our stations, to play a part in making these days memorable in the history of our race.'

WINSTON CHURCHILL,
ADDRESS TO THE BOYS OF HARROW SCHOOL
29 OCT 1941

What We Have Witnessed, Endured and Survived

Natural disasters, such as storms, drought etc., can occur any time and
have devastating consequences on homes. National or world events can leave
an impact on every family – these need not be disasters but of historical
importance, such as the first man in space, the landing on Mars, or new inventions
that will affect the lives of every one of us.

'Nothing ever becomes real till it is experienced, even a proverb
is no proverb to you till your life has illustrated it.'

JOHN KEATS, LETTERS

'The horror of that moment,' the King went on, 'I shall never, never forget!'
'You will, though,' the Queen said, 'If you don't make a memorandum of it.'

LEWIS CARROLL, THROUGH THE LOOKING GLASS

Family Traditions, Anecdotes and Things to Remember

'Accidents will occur in the best-regulated families.'

CHARLES DICKENS, DAVID COPPERFIELD

'Where shall I begin, please your Majesty?' he asked.
'Begin at the beginning,' the King said, gravely, 'and go on till you come to the end: then stop.'

LEWIS CARROLL, THROUGH THE LOOKING-GLASS

Family Heirlooms

Object _____

History _____

_____

_____

Value _____

Object _____

History _____

_____

_____

Value _____

Object _____

History _____

_____

Value _____

'I love it, I love it; and who shall dare
To chide me for loving that old arm-chair?'

ELIZA COOK, THE OLD ARM-CHAIR

OBJECT

HISTORY

VALUE

OBJECT

HISTORY

VALUE

OBJECT

HISTORY

VALUE

OBJECT _____

HISTORY _____

_____

_____

VALUE _____

OBJECT _____

HISTORY _____

_____

_____

VALUE _____

'Keep the young generations in hail,
And bequeath them no tumbled house!'

GEORGE MEREDITH, THE EMPTY PURSE

OBJECT _____

HISTORY _____

_____

_____

VALUE _____

First published in the United Kingdom in 1995 by
Ebury Press Stationery
Random House, 20 Vauxhall Bridge Road, London SW1V 2SA
Random House UK Limited Reg. No. 954009

3 5 7 9 10 8 6 4 2
Copyright © Random House UK Ltd 1995

Colour illustrations from the collection of Archie Miles

All rights reserved. No part of this book may be reproduced
in any form or by any means without permission in writing
from the publisher.

Set in ITC Century Light Condensed

Printed and bound in Singapore

Designed by Nigel Partridge

ISBN 0 09 179097 2